Exploring the
CHESAPEAKE BAY

PEOPLE OF
THE CHESAPEAKE BAY

By Kathleen Connors

Gareth Stevens
Publishing

Please visit our website, www.garethstevens.com. For a free color catalog of all our high-quality books, call toll free 1-800-542-2595 or fax 1-877-542-2596.

Library of Congress Cataloging-in-Publication Data

Connors, Kathleen.
People of the Chesapeake Bay / by Kathleen Connors.
   p. cm. — (Exploring the Chesapeake Bay)
Includes index.
ISBN 978-1-4339-9777-8 (pbk.)
ISBN 978-1-4339-9778-5 (6-pack)
ISBN 978-1-4339-9776-1 (library binding)
1. Chesapeake Bay (Md. and Va.)—Juvenile literature. I. Connors, Kathleen. II. Title.
F187.C5 C66 2014
975.2—d23

First Edition

Published in 2014 by
Gareth Stevens Publishing
111 East 14th Street, Suite 349
New York, NY 10003

Designer: Andrea Davison-Bartolotta
Editor: Kristen Rajczak

Photo credits: Cover, p. 1 Cavan Images/Iconica/Getty Images; pp. 4–5, 16–17 (background) iStockphoto/Thinkstock; p. 5 (top) courtesy of NASA; p. 5 (bottom) Karl Musser/Wikimedia Commons; p. 6 Chip Somodevilla/Getty Images; p. 7 (inset) courtesy of Bureau of Land Management; p. 7 (main) Theodore de Bry/The Bridgeman Art Library/Getty Images; pp. 8–9 Marilyn Angel Wynn/Nativestock/Getty Images; p. 9 (inset) Wikimedia Commons; p. 10 Thomas J. Abercrombie/National Geographic/Getty Images; p. 11 Archive Photos/Getty Images; pp. 12–13 Historic Map Works LLC/Getty Images; p. 15 (main) Myron Davis/Time Life Pictures/Getty Images; p. 15 (inset) Darren Brode/Shutterstock.com; p. 17 (map) courtesy of Chesapeake Bay Program; p. 19 Karen Bleier/AFP/Getty Images; p. 20 Greg Pease/The Image Bank/Getty Images; p. 21 Lloyd Fox/Baltimore Sun/MCT via Getty Images; p. 22 Sarah L. Voisin/The Washington Post via Getty Images; p. 23 Kenneth K. Lam/Baltimore Sun/MCT via Getty Images; p. 24 Stephen St. John/National Geographic/Getty Images; pp. 24–25 Mark Wilson/The Boston Globe via Getty Images; p. 26 USAF/Getty Images; p. 27 Joshua Roberts/Bloomberg via Getty Images; p. 28 Greg Pease/Photographer's Choice/Getty Images; p. 29 Simon Bruty/Sports Illustrated/Getty Images.

Printed in the United States of America

CPSIA compliance information: Batch #CS13GS: For further information contact Gareth Stevens, New York, New York at 1-800-542-2595.

CONTENTS

Words in the glossary appear in **bold** type the first time they are used in the text.

THE MAIN ATTRACTION

From fisherman to fighter pilots, the people who live and work in the Chesapeake Bay region are as **unique** as the bay itself! The Chesapeake Bay is an estuary, which is a body of water where the salt water of the ocean meets freshwater from inland. The freshwater comes from thousands of **tributaries** that empty into the bay, including the major river systems of the York, the James, the Susquehanna, the Rappahannock, and the Potomac Rivers.

Abundant wildlife and water, transportation opportunities, and natural beauty have drawn people to the bay's shores for thousands of years. Today, the Chesapeake Bay **watershed** is one of the fastest growing regions in the United States.

Susquehanna River

Chesapeake Bay

COOPERSTOWN, NY ●

BINGHAMTON, NY ●

WILKES-BARRE, PA ●

HARRISBURG, PA ●

HAVRE DE GRACE, MD ●

MANY JOBS TO DO

Parts of six states make up the Chesapeake Bay watershed, including Maryland, Pennsylvania, Delaware, Virginia, New York, and West Virginia, as well as Washington, DC. The more than 17 million people who live in this area do a variety of jobs. Some of the biggest industries of the bay region include seafood production, manufacturing, agriculture, and government and military work.

Look how many cities and towns have grown up along the Susquehanna River! Even as far north as Cooperstown, New York, is considered part of the Chesapeake Bay watershed since the river empties into the bay.

NATIVE AMERICAN HISTORY

As in many parts of the present-day United States, the Chesapeake Bay region was home to Native American tribes when European explorers and settlers arrived. In fact, these tribes' ancestors moved to the areas of Maryland and Virginia more than 10,000 years ago!

The Paleo-Indians were the earliest group to roam near the Chesapeake Bay. They probably hunted big animals. From about 9,000 to 3,000 years ago, Archaic Indians visited the bay to fish and perhaps even harvest oysters! The Woodland Indians were the first to build settlements near the bay. These villages moved every few years to use new plots of land for farming.

MODERN CHICKAHOMINY TRIBE MEMBER

TRIBES TODAY

Native Americans still make up a small part of the population in the Chesapeake Bay region. More than 40,000 people in Maryland identify as Native American, though only two tribes are officially recognized—the Piscataway Indian Nation and Piscataway Conoy Tribe. Virginia recognizes 11 tribes, including the Chickahominy, Mattaponi, and Patawomeck.

While the earliest Native American tribes didn't leave written records to confirm their presence near the bay, they did leave tools, bones, and pots. Archaeologists have found these and figured out how old they are!

These early people chose to settle around the Chesapeake Bay for its bounty of wildlife, such as the many fish in the bay and its tributaries. They also found good farmland, plants that could be eaten, and an ideal place to launch their canoes. They used the connected waterways of the bay watershed for transportation.

By 1600, three main tribes lived around the Chesapeake Bay—the Nanticoke, Piscataway, and Powhatan. One powerful chief, Wahunsonacock, overtook and joined together several tribes to form a confederacy, or united group, throughout the Virginia area known as Tidewater. He was called Powhatan, a name taken from his people and home village.

FIRST, THE SPANISH

The first Europeans sailed into the bay during the mid-1500s. Some historians say that around 1560, Spanish explorers kidnapped a Powhatan boy, probably to be an interpreter once he learned his captors' language. He may have returned to Virginia with Spanish **missionaries** about 10 years later, when they built a mission on the York River. The Powhatans attacked it in 1571 and killed the missionaries.

POWHATAN

The Nanticoke, Piscataway, and Powhatan tribes spoke similar languages. They worked together to face the colonists—though most of them were forced to move or died from war and disease within 100 years of the first European settlement of the area.

THE BRITISH ARE COMING!

The Chesapeake Bay region became the location of the first successful permanent English settlement for many of the same reasons Native American tribes lived there—water, transportation, possible farmland, and a ready source of food. The colony of Jamestown was founded on the James River in 1607.

Captain John Smith, a leader in the colony, made a map of the Chesapeake Bay soon after Jamestown's founding. While exploring the area around the bay, Smith was captured by Chief Powhatan! This encounter led to a peaceful agreement between the two groups, but it didn't last. Attacks from both sides occurred through the mid-1600s.

STATUE OF JOHN SMITH IN JAMESTOWN, VIRGINIA

THE LOST COLONY: ROANOKE

The first English colony was founded on Roanoke Island in present-day North Carolina. About 600 colonists sailed over in 1585 to the land the English called Virginia. After a big storm, most returned to England. A small number remained in the colony. However, when an English ship sailed to the Roanoke colony in 1590, no one remained. Were they killed by a nearby tribe? Did they move? No one is sure!

John Smith wrote a lot about the native people he met. His journals have helped historians learn more about the tribes.

GROWTH AROUND THE BAY

Though the first years of Jamestown Colony were hard, by 1750, about 380,000 people lived near the Chesapeake Bay! Slaves and European **immigrants** made up a large part of the growing population. Many worked on the plantations and smaller farms that grew crops such as the cash crop tobacco.

Germans from Pennsylvania, as well as French and Welsh immigrants, made their way into Maryland and Virginia during the 1700s. Around the 1840s, Irish, Poles, Italians, and Greeks had all become part of a growing melting pot on the Chesapeake Bay's shores—especially in Baltimore, Maryland! Though it had become a city less than 50 years before, Baltimore was the second-largest US city in 1840.

POPULATION BOOMS, ECONOMY BLOOMS

By the 1800s, agriculture, the slave trade, and transportation through the Chesapeake Bay's many waterways had made the region prosperous. The British targeted it during the War of 1812 because the bay had become a center of trade and shipbuilding, as well as government. In 1800, the US capital was established in Washington, DC, on the Potomac River, a tributary of the bay!

Norfolk (shown here) and Richmond, Virginia, were also growing cities around the bay during the mid-1800s.

The population of the Chesapeake Bay watershed doubled between 1950 and 2011. Baltimore continues to be one of the largest cities. It was one of the country's top 20 most populous cities in every **census** until 2000. More than 620,000 people live in Baltimore. Almost 64 percent are black, and the growing group of Latino Americans makes up 4.2 percent of the population.

In the 2010 census, the **metropolitan area** made up of Washington, DC, and Arlington and Alexandria, Virginia, was the seventh-most populous in the United States. Between 2000 and 2010, the population grew by about 785,000 people! Today, the population is more than 5.5 million.

POPULATION CENTERS

Baltimore and Washington, DC, may be the most populous cities in the bay watershed, but they aren't the only major ones! Newport News, Virginia—found right at the mouth of the Chesapeake Bay—is home to about 180,000 people. Smaller populated areas can be found on the tributaries leading into the bay, too. The Choptank River begins in Kent County, Delaware. Kent County has about 162,000 residents.

The US census gathers **demographic** information about the country every 10 years. That's how we know about how many people identify as a certain race, or how many men and women live in a place.

United States' Census

Use a blue or black pe

Start he

Census must c
tes on April 1,
answ
his h
mos

15

CHESAPEAKE BAY WATERSHED POPULATION (2010)

The population map on page 17 shows the entire Chesapeake Bay watershed. The most populous areas are near the bay and around Washington, DC. Use the colors in the map key to see how many people live near you!

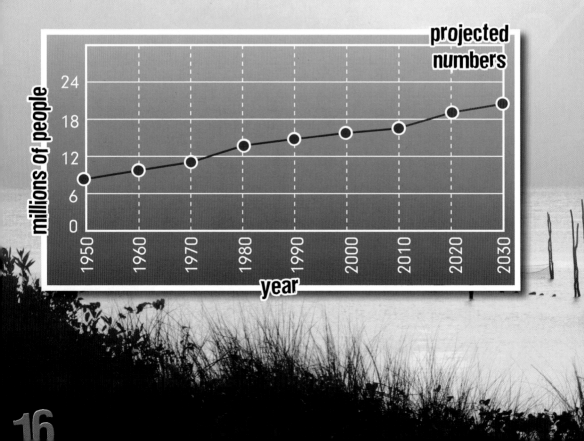

projected numbers

millions of people

24

18

12

6

0

1950 1960 1970 1980 1990 2000 2010 2020 2030

year

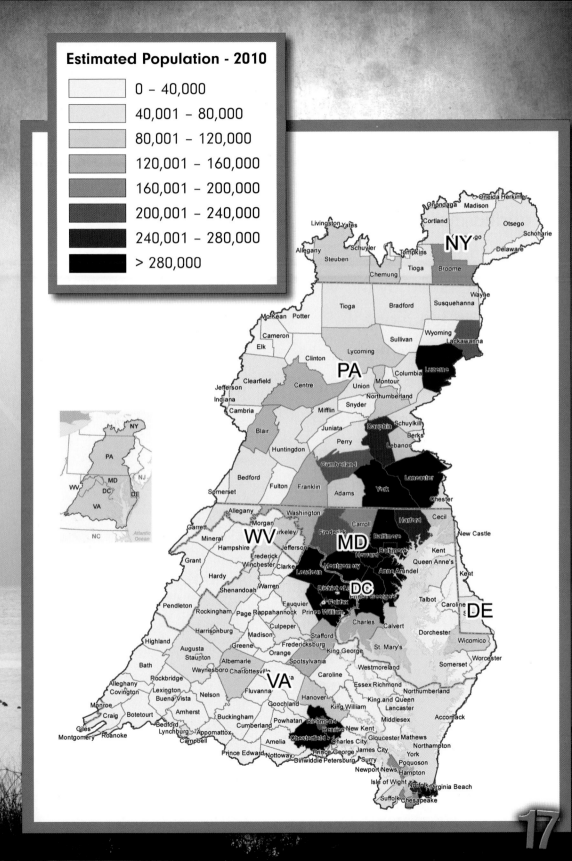

Estimated Population - 2010

- 0 – 40,000
- 40,001 – 80,000
- 80,001 – 120,000
- 120,001 – 160,000
- 160,001 – 200,000
- 200,001 – 240,000
- 240,001 – 280,000
- > 280,000

TOO MANY PEOPLE?

Every state in the Chesapeake Bay watershed grew in population from 2000 to 2010. Virginia alone added more than 920,000 people! Some people think that as many as 20 million people may live in the watershed by the year 2030—and they argue that might be too many.

Why does the Chesapeake Bay continue to draw new residents? It has continued to grow and change as the world around it does. From recognizing that investing in **conservation** can help the economy, to bringing in new industries, the people of the Chesapeake Bay region are taking charge of their own future!

IMMIGRATION

Immigration is one major way the population in the Chesapeake Bay watershed continues to grow. A study published in 2010 reported that immigration accounted directly for 40 percent of the population growth in the watershed between 2000 and 2009. That number increased to 66 percent when children born to immigrants in the United States were included. About 98 percent of Maryland's population growth came from immigration!

Many groups say the bay cannot support such a large population. The more people who move to the watershed, the more pollution will be produced and the more forests and wetlands will be cleared for building.

BAY VALUE

The people of the Chesapeake Bay watershed work in many industries. Some depend on the bay, while others don't. However, most industries in the watershed affect the bay, either because they bring more people to the area, cause pollution, or use some of the area's **natural resources**. Power companies, for example, use a lot of water from the bay.

Large parts of the population have jobs in manufacturing. In Maryland, this includes electronics, chemicals, and items used in transportation. Altogether, the many industries of the Chesapeake Bay may be worth more than $1 trillion! Read on to find out more about some of the coolest bay-based industries.

AIR POLLUTION PRODUCED BY A PLANT IN BALTIMORE

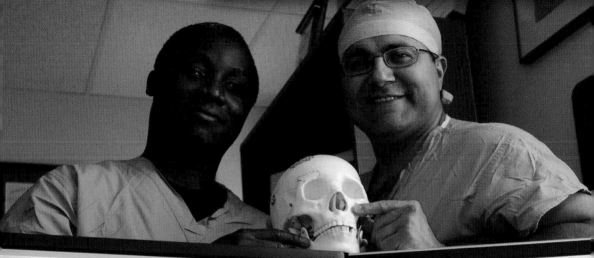

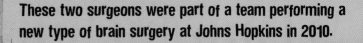
These two surgeons were part of a team performing a new type of brain surgery at Johns Hopkins in 2010.

WHERE THEY WORK

The Chesapeake Bay area has a booming **technology** industry, especially around Washington, DC, and Richmond, Virginia. Maryland also has become known as a great place to work in aerospace and information technology. Many people are also employed in health care and education, two industries with lots of research opportunities. Known for its medical breakthroughs, Johns Hopkins University is in Baltimore.

INDUSTRY STARTS EARLY

Since the mid-1700s, commercial fishing has been a huge industry around the Chesapeake Bay. More than 40,000 people work in the seafood industry, which produces more than 500 million pounds of seafood each year! Maryland produces the most crabs in the country. Fishermen who work on and around the bay also bring in flounder, bass, menhaden, and clams.

The Chesapeake Bay Foundation reported this industry brings in about $2 billion a year. Oysters once accounted for a good deal of that income. Low oyster populations brought about by disease, bad water quality, and overharvesting have caused Virginia and Maryland to lose more than $4 billion in the last 30 years.

FISH PROTECTION

Overfishing, pollution, and diseases have troubled populations of commercially harvested fish since settlers first came to the area. Today, harvesting limits protect populations that have greatly decreased over the years. Conservation is important to the health of the bay itself—and to the Chesapeake Bay region's economy. For example, declining populations led to a 40 percent decrease in crabbing jobs in Maryland and Virginia between 1998 and 2006.

Watermen, or those who fish or harvest crabs and oysters, often work for themselves. There are also big companies that catch fish on the Chesapeake Bay.

Early in their history, both Virginia and Maryland had economies based in agriculture—especially tobacco. Farms have changed a lot since then! The Chesapeake Bay region is home to family farms, which might be just a few hundred acres, and huge farms run by big businesses. Maryland produces soybeans and corn. In Virginia, tobacco is still grown, but poultry, cattle, grains, and some vegetables are the state's main products.

About one-fourth of the bay watershed is used for agriculture today. However, in Maryland and Virginia, it's only a small part of the economy, and fewer people work in agriculture than other industries.

SOYBEAN FIELD

POLLUTION SOLUTION?

Both crop and livestock farming in the Chesapeake Bay watershed cause pollution. **Runoff** from chemicals used in growing crops ends up in the water! But about half of the pollutants in the bay come from the waste of cows and other livestock. Some farmers are trying to cut down on their impact. Streambank fencing and "buffer" trees keep livestock out of waterways leading to the bay.

Farmers in the Chesapeake Bay watershed may plant cover crops, or crops planted after a field is harvested, to stop excess soil and other matter from ending up in the Chesapeake Bay.

From shipbuilding to the manufacture of military technology, a big part of the Chesapeake Bay economy is tied to the US military. The Norfolk Naval Station houses the largest group of US Navy forces in the world. The marine corps, coast guard, and air force all have stations near the bay, too. The US Department of Defense employs many people in Virginia and works with many businesses around the state.

Of course, with the nearness of the nation's capital, that's not the only government work in the Chesapeake area. A large part of the population near the Chesapeake Bay works for the US government!

DC COMMUTERS

The population of Washington, DC, increases by more than 70 percent each day with commuters, or those who travel into the city to work. The cost of living in Washington, DC—in addition to its limited land area—causes many to live in other parts of the Chesapeake Bay region. They often use a combination of driving and public transportation to get to work and back home each day.

THE PENTAGON

Shipbuilding near the Chesapeake Bay dates back hundreds of years. Today, Baltimore and Hampton Roads, Virginia, are still some of the busiest ports on the East Coast.

BE A TOURIST!

The Chesapeake Bay watershed is full of great places to visit from top to bottom! Tourism, the business of bringing in and entertaining visitors, is a big industry around the Chesapeake Bay. It brings in billions of dollars a year and provides many jobs to those who live in the region. In 2010, about 350,000 people were working in the tourism industry in Virginia.

So, what do tourists like to do? With all the bay's waterways, fishing is a popular sport in the watershed! Historical sites such as famous battlefields and Fort McHenry near Baltimore Harbor are also big draws.

THOMAS POINT
SHOAL LIGHTHOUSE

FAMOUS FACES

Many important historical figures have hailed from the Chesapeake Bay region. George Washington's home, Mount Vernon, is found in Virginia along the Potomac River—a tributary of the bay! Harriet Tubman was born in Maryland. She escaped slavery and led many other slaves to freedom during the mid-1800s. Thurgood Marshall, the first African American Supreme Court justice, lived in Baltimore.

Boating in the beautiful waters of the Chesapeake Bay is a favorite tourist pastime.

GLOSSARY

census: a count of population. It's taken every 10 years in the United States.

conservation: the care of the natural world

demographics: the features of a population

immigrant: one who comes to a new country to settle there

metropolitan area: a major city and its surrounding suburbs and towns

missionary: someone who travels to a place to spread their faith

natural resource: things in nature that can be used by people

runoff: the rain or other precipitation that drains into a river or stream, usually carrying with it dissolved waste or other material

technology: the practical application of specialized knowledge, especially in the production or use of electronics and computers

tributary: a stream or river flowing into a larger body of water

unique: one of a kind

watershed: the whole area that drains into a body of water

FOR MORE INFORMATION

Books

Bennett, Doraine. *Coastal Plain (Tidewater)*. Hamilton, GA: State Standards Publishing, 2011.

Lusted, Marcia Amidon. *America's Colonization and Settlement: 1585–1763*. Ann Arbor, MI: Cherry Lake Publishing, 2011.

Ransom, Candice F. *Why Did English Settlers Come to Virginia? And Other Questions About the Jamestown Settlement*. Minneapolis, MN: Lerner Publications, 2011.

Websites

Captain John Smith Chesapeake National Historic Trail: The American Indians
www.smithtrail.net/native-americans/
Learn more about the Native Americans who lived in the Chesapeake Bay area before settlers came.

Chesapeake Bay: Our History and Our Future
www.marinersmuseum.org/sites/micro/cbhf/index.html
Read about the history and growth of the Chesapeake Bay region on the website of the Mariner's Museum, which you can also visit in Newport News, Virginia.

INDEX